A

GERRY MCGRATH was born i　　　　　　　　　　　　 ᴜ 1962
and studied at Strathclyde University before becoming a teacher. He
received a Robert Louis Stevenson Memorial Award in 2004.

GERRY McGRATH

A to B

CARCANET

First published in Great Britain in 2008 by
Carcanet Press Limited
Alliance House
Cross Street
Manchester M2 7AQ

The lines in 'Calling' 'I was twelve the first time I walked / on water.' quote the
opening sentence of *Mr Vertigo* by Paul Auster, published by Faber and Faber Ltd,
and are reproduced by kind permission of the publisher.

A CIP catalogue record for this book is available from the British Library
ISBN 978 1 85754 877 8

The publisher acknowledges financial assistance from Arts Council England

Typset in Bembo by XL Publishing Services, Tiverton
Printed and bound in England by SRP Ltd, Exeter

For Kate

How short became the road
That seemed the longest.

Anna Akhmatova

Acknowledgements

I would like to express my gratitude to:

The Scottish Arts Council and National Library of Scotland who enabled me to spend two months at the Hotel Chevillon, Grez-sur-Loing, in November 2004 and April 2005 as a Robert Louis Stevenson Memorial Fellow.
Margareta Persson.
Donal McLaughlin.
David Kinloch.
Mme Bernadette Plissart.
Adam Fleck.

Contents

III

I

Higher

So, this evening ends on a palette
of leaves, flushed lilac sky, bramble
punnet dwindling to a shadow of itself
in the darkening heat

while above the city
the forgetful droning of a pencil-thin
aircraft climbing higher and higher
drains away all resistance.

No End of Exile

In a house
on the outskirts
of Perpignan
at a funny angle
to the rest of Spain
the man who never was
a Spanish Republican
sits in full view
of the old country.

His dog welcomes us.
His wife since 1939 says hello.
Where he looks out
grass the colour of nicotine
stands taller than the mountains.

I became a florist, he tells you.
Flowers called me: *what kept you
all these years?*
I wasn't listening, but I am now.

The dog is sprawled on the floor.
Anastasia sits in exile
at the table in a corner of the room.
Fresh-cut flowers here
there and everywhere unite
the furniture.

Perdoneme, Manolo says.
Sometimes I forget myself.

Magpie

The magpie stands to the side,
sucks in its cheeks, calls.

There are times I need
to chase down the old life
not climb over
or tunnel under it
but take its weight and shudder.

Times I'd like to ask that bird
how it gained its loneliness
how it got to be how it is
fixing things with that one eye
like a dark moon.

Steady

Since then they have come at the rate
of one a day. A rough, ballpark figure,
but honest. Is it luck, or a turnaround
in fortunes? I hope so. Where they spring
from God knows. I just remember the day
it all started, being so glad it was the month
when things start to happen. Blue and green.
A certain blossoming. Warming baths of air.
I have no right to say this but yes they come,
like questions from children, with equal amounts
of trust and worry. That's it, *trust*. You are
entrusted. After all this time, what you've done,
others waiting for the 'big fall'. Now. Go ahead.
Take the gate off its latch, run, feel the grass like
a cradle beneath your feet, generous and cool from
heel to toe, keeping you steady. Who knows what will
crop up in the future? But for now, go, play, live.

Sycamores

Standing in
out the downpour
he nods upwards
to the gossamer rain
beading down.

Forget the old life.
Yesterday. The future
lies somewhere
in the afternoon.

★

Later, watching the wind
lift the sycamores.
Everyone he loved he left.

Weight

Met by fog today and the remains of a frost
on the leaves and windscreens. Never mind
that yesterday the barber got it all wrong and
the book of Milosz's poems still hasn't arrived.
Never mind. Was it a year ago or last night
you bit me on the earlobe? Kissed me on the lips
and held me? I can still feel your weight.
A snell October wind finds the bruise, has me
tucking my head to the right, smiling. Everything.
Everything's a blur.

A Question

Wake up, baffled, from where sleep
took you to last night and glimpse
in a daze of rain the young couple,
in matching jackets, heading for
the park, arm–in–arm, obscured now
by a flurry of leaves that are the colour
of fresh, peeled ginger root.
You mouth the words through the liquid
glass: may they remain that way.
May they love each other ceaselessly,
without quarter, even if it kills them.
Alone, you raise a hand up your back
and feel at where nails tore flesh last night.
Why do you do it? It's a question you ask all
day, searching with watertight fingers for the
answer.

Sleep Alights

The earth
shows a grey flank
to the moon.

Old Brain, he says,
toothpaste in one hand,
rubbing down that face
with the other.
*Old Brain is rattling
in its cage.*

Still
no matter what
he is up.

And the sun also rose
today.

Baby Spuds

Two days ago, for example. After the showers that their friends
insisted they should come and have, if the need arose. Well, it did.
So they went. Had dinner, too. Roast chicken and cauliflower
cheese, caramelised carrots and boiled baby spuds. Gravy.
The red wine flowed. Water came out a frosted jug. They got
round to talking, about death and finality, mostly.
But the saddest thing he heard all night, definitely, wasn't
the floorboards, or the creak of the panelled door swinging
on its hinges, or the racket the tortoise cat made on the landing.
It was this: *we're just language*. He could've gret. Tell the truth,
despite the good times, maybe even believed it.

Early Flowers

March. Winter over and no one can remember
blue skies like it. The early flowers are out.
Birds are singing in the evening. It's light
till six and beyond. In a week or two the clocks
will leap forward.

Yesterday I returned a cd loan, but not before
I'd bought a tape and taped it.
It's on now. Side A of the last of the last
quartets. Far away I am listening.

Overnight

Springday like a tusk. Buds at last
have outrun the long-distance winter
to push through.
Snowdrops, crocuses, daffodil stems
quake like cowards in a pale springlight
that has settled like overnight rain
on the garden's top lip.

In No Time

Clyde Falls in May dense sunlight soothing leaves
the low conversation of water we walk on
your hand in mine come across the signs for falcons

follow on up the path to where a warden trains
his glasses on the nest hands them to us
points to where a mother and her young

walking back we hold each other but tighter now
shouts singing wolf-whistles come from the boys
across the river same ones we saw on the way up
let them sing dance show their backsides all night
if they want

in no time at all the path shallows the water broadens
voices peel away to our amazement there is a silence
of squirrels

Only Life

1

Lint glimmers
dull in the baubled wool;
laundered stars unsparkled
blink on
off   on

2

In a voice
surprised
by its own remoteness
my father not knowing
he was entering
his final month
winked

                           cigarette

butt clamped
in the jaws of his fingers
and said
precisely

precisely

as if there was something
extraordinary
absolutely extraordinary
and memorable
about this
his only life.

A Man Unable

Noticing a man unable
to gather the softness of a pup
up in his arms, I looked again
at the animal, at the curve of
its slinking away, slinked–back
ears. From this slow retreat a single
forepaw inched skywards. Immediately
the pup was swept up. Cuddled, loved
beyond love, reason; held above
the rig of buildings to the sun. So small,
it fitted in to the high country, the high
pocket of a short-sleeved summer shirt.
From there, shivering, it chased the nodding
world, this world, and the next and the next,
scenting each and every rare grass blade, as if
shaken by its origins on the homeward road,
shaken to its root.

II

Pointing North

Frequent showers
mean the room blushes
then turns pale
in quicker than quick
succession. It's
while I'm watching all this
going on
the little starling re-appears.
Watchful, it travels back and
forth, smuggling food
to its young
who are in a nest somewhere
inside the wall.

Tolstoy was wrong about Chekhov
but he didn't care. Last
Saturday I saw a fledgling
by the kerb, skin all pink
and tough, like chewing gum.
The little yellow nib of a beak
pointing north.
The first thing I thought about
was the starling and its chorus of chicks,
then about beautiful days. Then Time.
Then poetry. History.
In that order.

The Colour of Water

On glassy Turnberry beach
we went looking
for a world without stars.
From sand you magicked
a castle; moat, portcullis,
ramparts, turrets
ie the lot
while my cheap feet made
do with carving the date
and our names
beside a feathery burn.

See, poetry, what you can do
when you try?
If I was feeling brave, poetic,
painterly, I might say:
take one potato (halved)
a few watercolours
and attempt to draw
this threesome –

hand that weighs, judges
man's equine shiver
a charnel house of shells

Dry Flood

Today unlike yesterday
the wind was only audible
as rain bundling into trees.
Understudy, it mouthed
its lines behind wet lips. But
yesterday was another story.
A dry flood, it turned leaves
silver, dented fields of grass.
Dwarves had to hold on to their hats.
Zany butterflies beat their wings
inside the stomachs of giants.
It was something, to say the least.
Bats were phoning their friends up.
The earth plugged an ear, hummed
a foreign tune. Schubert quintet.
Rain when it fell, hardly disquieted
the fish basking in glimmery shadows.
Then the wind died. Covered its mouth.
Tomorrow was suddenly unploughable.
Everyone stood on one leg, with one eye
looking over their shoulder, waiting
for Time to do the same.

Phenomenon

The oregano, rosemary plants we bought
look a million miles from anywhere
shivering in the terracotta pot they share
on the window ledge.
It's evening, about 8. The arthritic dog's
just barked twice. Magpie's loitering
on the triangular wall. Clouds
lie like salmon.
This is the picture, except for the phenomenon
of the two trees. One catches the sun, fizzes.
The other is cider-apple red, sleepy.
I'm thinking *nothing can beat this*
but I'm also thinking
that in a couple of hours from now
the moon will show its face
and play the card
it keeps forever in its palm.

True Air

July and from the kitchen window I see
the tallest of the copper beeches burst open
and a school of pigeons spill out; the true air
surrounding a man puffed up in a yellower
than yellow jacket; an L-plated seagull
preparing for take-off, unpacking its wings,
dusting off its feet on an unremembered statue
before falling headlong on gravity, soaring
light over the pastry roofs, open-bound.

Midsummer

I wanted to send you a poem today.
A poem with night and day in it, but
above all day. A poem unlike the next
one that I'm going to write, about climbing
Earl's Seat, about getting lost, found,
about the scree and how the hills look
different up there. About the man with
his young son, the man who wanted
to know the time, the picnickers who looked
as if they'd been expecting us. About how
later, we lay in bed, our faces close, burning,
deepening, so close, as close as the midsummer
sky and dark buildings ever are.

Busy

i.m. Roma Stephenson

If it had been thirty years ago say, the seventies,
I might have said you leapt higher than the phone
when it rang. But no, this conversation started and
finished and I could tell from your face that what
your mother had to say about your grandmother wasn't all
good news. Age, infirmity, depression, were all getting
the better of her, pulling her down.
The old woman just wanted to go to sleep and not
wake up again. I noticed this.
When you'd done listening, talking, you uncradled
the phone from under your chin and sighed, a long deep sigh.
You came and lifted the towel from around my shoulders,
flapped it – hair-clippings went flying out – and re-arranged
it in a fashion over me. Then you went and stood behind and
were quiet. For a while absolutely nothing happened. Looking
out the kitchen window I missed the sound of the clippers
picking up where they'd left off. Hair began to fall again, in
swaths, curls, wet black snow landing on the floorboards.
I kept looking out. The evening was so languid. The breeze
of earlier on had died down. Curtains hung limp, slightly
open. The sky was losing its heat. I could make out
just and no more the beginnings of the deepest blue, one
or two stars alight in the darkness that wasn't quite darkness,
and feel your busy hands, your thoughts more than decades away.

Secrets

The one-eyed poet
stares at nothing
then picks nothing up,
turns it in his hand
until it bleeds a secret.
                    Out there
among the bronze shields
of summer, ticker-tape
pigeons flicker. Starlings
tip their wings. A gull
alone in its cockpit
sifts high
above the ocean of trees.

Old Masters

Remember today, how we saw no fog, just
high grey cloud trailing its rainy legs
across the Old Kilpatrick crags, crop fields
the colour of egg yolk, a mussel-blue sky.
The young couple killing themselves
laughing at something or other. Blind girl,
her mother and father, standing outside BHS,
leafing through her repertoire of songs.
And the masters, of course, the Dutch masters.
Helmet, breastplate, light. All that. All that.

Gift

for Stella Rotenberg

Poetry puts air our way,
allows us the feel
of a fur hat inside a fur coat,
to observe tiny immensities
with eyes like sharks.
It brings knowledge
and understanding that
gentleness somehow endures,
that our lives, sweet breathable
lives, are scent and honey.

Limits

You would hear waves
pound the shore
see birds flash and drop
like stones

you would watch the sky
turn truer than true
a thin viscous catch
of gold, powder-blue
     yet

you would let me be

conceal nothing
that is not
your privacy.

Whispers

From a table; lone, polished, walnut table with history, I unhook
and hook eyes on the drowsy sailcloth of your skin, watch you
walking in the shadowless hall, clothes for the basket, hesitating.
And what I would like to do is part company with this dreary
chair, get up, hold you, kiss you, but outside a wind is busy piling
leaves against the gable, rain's whispering in the dark, and the
promise of what might be is looking back at us through a doorway
with eyes like wet, black earth.

Anstruther

How, where, does it begin?
In the head? With the
extremities? You countable,
lovable digits, you fingers, toes,
are you where it all starts?
Make a note: the train leaves
at 9.10 in the morning,
for a city in a valley. I don't
know its name, who lives there.
No one does. There are old stories.
Many have lived remarkable lives.

Sawdust beach, amber moon,
sea moss, sifting herons,
lemony lime, piglet spill,
crimson rock pools reflecting
things beyond reflection.

We fish for others.
We trespass.
We are beloved.

Dead House

Earplugs, what can I say?
What can I tell you?
A mouse roared and silence
caught you up. Goodbye!

Don't worry about me.
I'll be busy, looking at shadows,
listening to the music, speaking
without reply.

What time is it? It's five
o'clock in the morning.
What am I doing? I'm up,
going through this house
of the dead, one room at a time,
wondering why, after so much
noise, all that's left is quiet.

Same Bird

Down it came again this evening
from the rooftop shadows all shadows
lost

same flesh nerves blue-black feathers
orange beak
alive to its own span
a blackness deepening

same bird

getting older in the last rays of the sun
in the first words of a diffident moon.

Shape of a Chair

After sleep he wakes again
to that world – orange light
finding a landscape
in the shape of a chair,
yesterday's clothes, clock,
arms, cheeks, eyelids, nose.
Lie still, the small voice
whispers. You are also
being remembered.

Anklet

Fleas are biting hard. Suspicious
of ghosts, the critic ponders
the 'ongoing project of Modernism'.
Mother listens to her son, is drawn
to the unthinkable. Creatures,
the wee beggars, are invincible!

★

Words rise in the right silences
bringing him close, closer.

★

He hears the river at night
feels the little anklet of bites
sees the long white tooth
of the road stretching out.

★

And still wanting, moves on.

No Forgetting

When you look up say, sweetly smiling,
the dark corners of your mouth folded in,
there's no forgetting that important part of us
that remains.

Still

Waking before dawn, he heard
birdsong, got up. Feet on the verge
of cramping, he walked in darkness
through to the kitchen. There,
from the window, he focused first
on the tree, then the lamp, little
white globe in a mesh of branches,
shedding its light, enough to create
the illusion of a perfect cage, perfectly
circular, perfectly still.

Particles

Japanese businessman sings Sinatra.
Blackbirds are quelled by daybreak.
Pink flamingo curtains, muslin-made,
are hitched, harelipped, softly spoken
in softer light.
The sodium whiff of the body
rises.

                              Sleepless
click–cough–cry of a neighbour.

The far end of the room.
The bleed of the morning, antique
dancing, danced anew.
Cutlery, plates, pot, snowed with potato.
Streak of magpie, untamed lightning.
A man: white skin, whiter hair, blackest jacket.
A canal: shadows of trees competing for water
with ducks learning to land, their outspoken Vs
spread to the banks, adding their own nothings
to particles of grass.

Soft Tissue

From this low brae, a holding
station where shadows of cloud are all
that crosses the snow, I hear
the speech marks of tenderness
that unravel you, a too demanding
fear of nothing changing suddenly
changing into beauty and weightlessness,
while your face, soft tissue
of your beginning and your ending,
tilts at an unknown future, a forgotten past.

Among the Blue

Somehow I wish I could say
it was indifference not love
that found the co-ordinates
for cormorants among the blue
the blue-white gulls

tell you that we have lived once
and will not come this way again

say to you that so long as art
teaches languages of recovery
eternal reminders of morning
will grow on our sweat, spume,
tick softly on our lips, on our lips.

Calling

Mid–February, blossom is our
surprise – pink and white.
A tiny bird, lit on a branch, peers
at an empty kitchen window.

'I was twelve the first time I walked
on water.'

Going, so then, I am gone. As if for the
last time, will you kiss me, on the mouth.
Hard. Now and never again. Time to go, Love.
Everything's dust and the road's calling me.

Baci

On a train somewhere south of Bern, Switzerland
the beautiful Italian woman
with knees like emaciated skulls
drops the phone into her lap.
Out the window the valleys deepen,
grow darker, mountains stretch, not
not in an illusion of painting.
                I feel a nudge,
take the *baci* you offer me, unwrap
the carefully wrapped silver foil
(bite-size chocolate, for small mouths)
and turn the treasure rightways up to read:
no le juzgue a quien se ama,
do not judge the beloved,
                      eyes roam
to snowy peaks, a steel blue sky.
In these heights, in such depths, a possible light.
Ser amado. Only be loved. Beloved.

The Language of Pines

Here again, yes here, touched,
yes, by the future. Let me say

how we progressed down the hill
stepping from fog to visibility.

Listen, these eyes, heat, more-
than-blood warmth, feel

the minute forgiveness of rain,
unconfessable love, salt,

hear the language of pines,
soft bleating as of a child
all

the painstaking increments
of our descending.

The Water, the Shore

My mother confesses to being
no longer that sure underfoot.
Progressed from seventy-five
to seventy-six, she says, life is
strictly for the living.

Her fridge shivers to a halt.
Her dog, absorbed in the mystery
of a front paw, is inward-looking
                    but

when those eyes turn outwards
they see as if hearing beyond walls
the depths, the water, the shore
where today, joyously, she will run.

Invisible

for Ciara MacLaverty

You can avoid sadness.
You can make a headboard for your bed
of the steel-greyness
that could be

Three waves rippling
in the still-damp hair
of a water-softened man

The surprising skin
of a river, seen-through
by herons

Or just clouds approaching
with the ease of animals
not herded, not driven.

Brief Season

Today's over, the thyme lost
in its pot, looks for the sun
already in your skin. A fierce
brief season slips you in.
Somewhere has your name.

Tomorrow will open like a page,
travel on a bend of daylight
to yesterday's places transformed
in July's deep mirrors.

Watching Primrose

Come on, forget the raspberries, let's go,
let's watch the evening primrose
as it undresses, as it reveals all
to those who've run without shoes
to see the unbuttoning of lemon, pale-lemon
leaves.

This phenomenon, earthed so deep
in the storied soil, transforms oval mouths
to mini-dishes bright as chestnut husks.

And yet.

The dampness rises.
Someone shakes time from a watch.
Above the pear tree a moon waits to cross.
In the house, on a low table
                      raspberries
turn to blood in a bowl sealed off
with cellophane.

Dishwater

Your face
your hands
are aged by heat
& soap.

The word inconsolable
describes tonight.

Inconsolable

In time you'll forget
even this.

A Sense of Occasion

In the space of a day
he took a train journey
to buy meat

spotted a girl
with her tie on backwards
walking away

glanced at clouds
hesitating towards
America

wrote poetry that burned
the rules of syntax

joined battle
with jittery wasps

gripped the spinning table
in a house also spinning

took off his shoes

tasted disappointment
laced with orange juice

listened to gulls crying
arriving late for dinner

shared sleep
with apple-white
flesh
and
woke countless times
unrestored
once to the buzzing

of a twin-engined light
aircraft crossing a hole
in the sky

through which he could hear

the beautiful echo of nothing
that had anything to do
with him, not-him.

Promise

There's this poem that begins
with a vase, four stems standing
in water translucent as the flesh
of grapes. It speaks of mothers
lifting stones, forking over wrack,
searching the pelts of bees for signs
of their departed sons, and ends abruptly,
with a surprise dividend, a crash
of old glass, some coins, goodbyes,
a promise.

III

The Middle Distance

It doesn't take a heron, the shape
of a heron even
to give my ignorance away
my love of things
unclassified –

a silly shape, a comic-opera hen
knocking on the wood of a tree
shutting down for winter, leafless
save for the thin fringe
of what could be birds aflutter
on its summit –

love of a landscape retreating
into itself and always itself
no matter my love.

Small Fires

Wednesday morning and the walk down
through the garden to the water's edge.
This could become a regular occurrence.
The signs are all there.
The little white specks on the tongue
that say 'ulcer', a discovered tenderness
of the flesh on the inside of the mouth,
legs both working, taking the weight,
arms in order, not so stiff, so sore.
The day some way off, like table-silver
sunk in a clear, shallow river.

A Milky Sunlight

A fat policeman, eyes set high in his head, keeps
the body company. An expression of some sadness
wreathes his face. He is also watching his footing.
A second man, face contorted by the effort, helps
to guide the trolley over the gravel strewn with leaves.
It's hard work, this taking care of the dead.
The wheels are unreliable. They twist and stick
in the mud and stones, the rain-softened grass.
The corpse, small under a black covering, shudders.
From a window it's impossible to say whether this is
the body of a child or a woman.

★

Sky's lighter now. The morning haze and fog have lifted.
A milky sunlight's pushing through. A van backs slowly
into the yard, full of leaves and machinery. Four men get out.
Each quickly retrieves his equipment and straps it on. There's
a single, throttled roar; some leaves go flying up. Nods all round.
Then they head off in the direction of the river where they work
with some urgency, by mid-morning are gone.

Two Friends

In the morning they got up and walked to the supermarket,
the two friends. They bought water, in litre and a half bottles,
enough for a few days, splitting six-packs into bags. Then
walked the long way home, through the forest, via the canal.
A dozen times or more they paused to look at the water.
Those flimsy bags really cut to the bone. That afternoon, deep
in conversation, one of them at least knew all about it, felt
the fire in his hands that spoke for their efforts. Glancing down,
he saw nothing, of course. No bruises, not a scratch. Just skin
stretched paper-thin over knuckle.

Mint Tea

Deadlines meant Cagnat always rose early. He had
a house to pay for, bills to meet. Two beautiful children
and a beautiful wife who gutted herself laughing
when he showed her what they'd done while she was out
– the kids and him – to the so-so painting of a street.
C'est magnifique, she said, patting down the dogs.
Words cannot describe.
After dinner, over mint tea and chocolate, he got the books out,
                                                    his books –
Sherlock Holmes, One Hundred Dead Writers, Monte Cristo –
and cup in hand, he took the guests through the drawings, one by
                                                            one.

Blue Light

for Bernadette Plissart

He worked all day and in the evening went down to the river. It was remarkably mild for the time of year. The little white chair was there, under the chestnut trees. The dinghy lay on the grass, half-filled with fallen leaves and water. Determined to see his favourite reflection, of the oaks fanning out across the river, he made his way down to the bottom step and stood. Night was creeping from the ground. A light growing bluer hung in the chestnut trees. A group of swans flew past in the semi-darkness, so close. He couldn't say precisely when the rain began.

Basics

He took his father fishing, showed him all he knew about tying up and casting and reeling in. About keeping the rod low when you wanted to trail the spinner, and pulling back hard on a strike. The basics. His dad was happy. He had found something else to do with his time, such time as he had. Death was no barrier, either. He still fished. Took the rod from the cellar and walked down the road to the pier. There, he had the line set up in minutes, ready to go. He cast. Where the spinner hit the water, the water boiled. He waited and waited, remembered those times in his life when he'd needed luck and luck found him.

Morning

He raises a glass to the bricks, steps outside.
So many hundreds of pages are left behind
squeezed into that silent room.

In the cool morning air, the river's smoking.
He leans like a ladder against the chestnut tree
shaking in its armour.

A goose beats its wings under the bridge.
Leaves quiver in a breath of wind. It's this
quieter, earlier world he's listening to.

Forest Path

The path falls open at a page, silence comes forward
without a step, embraces us. Pure light folds back
and grainy light passes, like dark snow in a comet's tail,
furring the trees.

Shadows creep and shrink. The air's browned like an apple.
The forest is a city without weight, the path is a trampoline.
In the depths of oil and ore the bones of the earth spring back
under our shallow, pointing feet.

Bright Walkway

End of dusk's late lesson. In the sky's
picked bones crows thin out
in side-long galaxies. Light stops
at the window's edge.

There is no space here, no shadow,
only the poem grows, fantastically,
a walkway between syllables, bright
as a struck match.

The Painter

for Ray Rummukainen and Sari Laitinen

Something important begins
with a sigh

the walls of the studio absorb
the sunshine
the tree shakes off its mask

apricot light stands up
through the leaves and
reaches into the room

of the painter who's there
feeling his art like a glove
blue with memory.

Island

Mid-afternoon, river like an unlit ship.
A flotilla of geese arrives from the bridge,
they have heard the snowfall of bread
echoing down the hull.

There is a soft, grey light, as if
to say, 'we are living on an island',
we are surrounded by water here
so calm, so peaceful.

Currency

for David Kinloch

A day, beautiful, like no other. The sky, blue, clean-shaven.
Joseph Haydn stops, rubs his chin, remembering the man
who wanted him to go to London, who promised adoration,
wealth, *difference*. Haydn trained an eye on the horizon.
In this world where duty prevails and music exists he smiled,
suggested an exchange. The two men parted in the warmth
of friendship, one clutching a fine new razor, the other a partita
wrapped in the fond embrace of his deep, deep pocket.

Yellow Ticket

The following afternoon at four, H was in the garden, preparing the slow shot he'd talked about, the hotel at dusk. He wanted a new photo for his wall. We'd already been to his studio to see the others. They were all poster-size. One of them was of a girl in a tent. In another, a cow's head, dark and shiny, loomed between metal bars, a yellow ticket pinned to its ear. Now, from the slightly open window of our room, we could see him moving around under the tree, measuring the daylight with a meter and positioning his lamps. Occasionally great silver flashes lit up the gloom. There was a smell of wood smoke and burning leaves. The tree seemed to droop. H looked up at us from the lawn. He was waving his arms, shouting something we couldn't quite hear. It sounded like 'up, up, up'.

First Detail

for Margareta Persson

That afternoon, loving just being in this landscape,
you saw sunlight reflected in the last high leaves

discovered *Blacksvamp* in a shade of saplings
pale as the earth where quietly it takes root.

'Shaggy Mane': a black mushroom.

Introductions

You didn't sigh when night put on
your father's coat
or when you sat talking till late
with Niran
whose Tatar mother tongue
feels like my skin

she tells you
Stillness doesn't scare her
Silence turns a searchlight on the self–
it confronts.

So it is
with some love and a little desperation she survives
waiting for the caress of a leaf, pebble, reflector light
to introduce her to the future

A to B

Today I counted ten butterflies
on the road to Montigny.
In temperatures closer to May
an army of red-backed beetles
staggered in their armour.
A dead marten lay by the roadside
in a shadow of trees
the answer to everything
inscribed in the hiatus
of its little brown tongue.

But let me tell you about the butterflies.

Powder Blue

In a cone-shaped field
ringed by jagged boulders
that might once've been
the milk teeth of giants
he sat reading

the powder-blue book
two hundred pages long
sixty years deep

written by a poet
who drew the marrow from starlight
and lived.

Imaginable Longing

for Niran Baibulat

the old streets groan
the chocolate fields of Genevraye
are slow moving

slower than time
they wear a beautiful necklace
of ancient dust

★

on the second day God didn't call up water
it sprang from the imaginable longing of rocks
to become the ocean bed

Small Hand

Late home
the sun melting behind cloud
scent of flowers in the air

light growing greener
trees deepening
the garden so still

toys scattered abandoned
on the grass

laughter
and the conversation of neighbours
coming through the hedge

Mozart wafting from an upstairs window

on the back doorstep
a small hand in mine
saving me

First Love

Sunlight swarms around the head
of the boy who sits playing piano
on the kitchen table.

The back door moves slow as a glacier.
Through the indifferent windows
grass gathers each note that travels
soundlessly from his fingertips.

Lately

for Donal McLaughlin

Steer clear of the orange juice, my friend warns me.
It's good advice. Recently I've noticed changes in him. Okay,
he's a little bit heavier about the middle, but above all it's the eyes.
They look somehow older. The old certainty has gone. Yet,
could I begin to count the ways in which his life has improved lately?
So, when he uses the word *industrial*, I know that this man
I've known for twenty years is thinking that happiness must
in such difficult times belong to everyone.

Tilleul

A cool, bright April morning and the tea's dark,
darker than I remember. Body's quieter now
after the shakes.
My thoughts go back to our conversation last night
about expectations and privilege. But not for long.
The concentration is shot and there's so much to do.
I raise the cup to my lips, taste that hint of lime
without bitterness.

Around the Edge

It's hard to move in the kitchen tonight.
The best cups, plates, glasses all sit under cover
and mustn't be disturbed. So we make do
around the edge of the table. Take the knives
from the block and prepare our simple meal.
Some vegetables. Tomatoes. Spaghetti. Water.
There's enough food for anyone who wants it
but no one comes. We sit and laugh and talk.
Just the two of us. You and me. Something low
and jazzy plays on the radio. We begin to feel
almost alone. That word, *almost*.

Cities

Where this morning the trees stand windless
flame-straight as if drinking up the dark

daylight travels along the pews
to the deep-down eyes at rest under slums

of old leaves and new cities of saplings
the swarming grass-shoots.

White Rain

Soft, white rain seeps through the grille.
The birdcage is buoyant, its flowers not
for drowning yet – they sup and breathe
their fragrance under the window's chin.

On the clasped hands of a studio roof
chaffinches flail and squabble, trailing
their desperate syllables like hooks
through the green air.

The rain steals down. Slowly
the tiles in the courtyard are turning
a darker red.

In Loving Memory

Yesterday I took a walk along *Rue Wilson*
and turned left into the local cemetery.
Sun on my back, I wandered on the path
looking and reading the inscriptions.
The husband who sleeps eternally with his wife.
The son who fell in battle.
The woman mourned by her friends.
The Englishman who met his end in 1882.
All given shelter here, by death.
I left sniffing lemon rosemary picked
from a hedge fringing some decrepit graves,
thinking about this sweet life and the road ahead
stretching.

Younger

I tell you
the stars will come out tonight
high over the heads of the bikers
the cyclists' multi-coloured tops
the bartender's wife
the little girl who must be her daughter
the deaf mute
the fifty-something Swedish artist
the camera crew
the man walking the Newfoundland puppy
the fat pigeon tucked under the eaves
the inner thoughts of houses
the torched hay bales
the luminous night-fields
the sun-blushed patio
the sweet unfinished beer

over the young firmament
and the younger, reeling moon.

Green Shallows

On the bridge, leaning on the bones of your bike
you stand watching the river turn, fold, rise up
to kiss your eyes. The green shallows move deeply
in you. Patterns of lace and spume are already written
in your work. You don't know how or when or where.
Without that knowledge you travel light
through the streets of towns and villages, breathing
the free air freely, in something like madness and love.